Personal Peace

Prayers for Women of All Faiths

edited by Lori Strawn

© 2010
All Rights Reserved.

No part of this publication may be reproduced, stored in a retrieval system, or transmitted, in any form or by any means, electronic, mechanical, photocopying, recording, or otherwise, without the written permission of the author.

First published by Dog Ear Publishing
4010 W. 86th Street, Ste H
Indianapolis, IN 46268
www.dogearpublishing.net

ISBN: 978-160844-799-2

This book is printed on acid-free paper.

Printed in the United States of America

Table of Contents

Personal Peace 1
Radiant Morning! 2
I Am the Diamond 3
Journey = Destination 4
Ritual 5
Light in the Depths 6
Peacemakers 7
Amazed 8
Whatever May Come 9
Don't Doubt It 10
Promise of a New Day 11
Prism of Compassion 12
My Last Pity Party 13
Silent Partner 14
A.M. and P.M. 15
Me Time 16
Attention Shoppers 17
Give Me Shelter 18
Keeping Perspective 19
Intervention 20
Hearth and Home 21
Grateful Start 22
Doubt 23
Career Steps 24
Faith 25
Morning 26

One Soft and Certain Voice..27
Army of Hope...28
Tearing Down the Anger 29
Energy Rush..30
Unfolding..31
Faith Vs. Reason...32
Shout 33
Sacred Agent 34
Lost and Found 35
What Happened? 36
Listening for You 37
Sailing Forth 38
Simple Sign 39
Impossibly Alive 40
Name Changing...41
Next Opportunity 42
Ever-Present 43
A Marriage in Trouble 44
Granddaughter...45
Trying Times 46
Raging Heart..47
With Me 48
Sick and Tired 49
Open Soul Surgery 50
Miracles of Routine 51
Erasure 52
Forgive, Forget, Move On 53
M-Word 54
Soul of Philanthropy 55
One Hot Mama 56
Climbing Mountains...57
Waiters 58
Moving Mountains..59
Wrapping Up 60
Soul Mate...61

Rendering	62
Devastation	63
Question	64
Until	65
Rebirth	66
Make Life, Make Sense	67
Divine Timing	68
Sisters by Choice	69
Only Child	70
You Are There	71
Music Within	72
Perfect Victim	73
Abiding	74
Arms Around Me	75
Measure of Success	76
Off the Shelf	77
Fussing Over the Folks	78
Living Fully	79
Inertia	80
Momentum	81
I Am Ageless	82
Road Map	83
Finding Home	84
Free at Last!	85
Stuck in My Head	86
Reaching Up and Out	87
Workplace Hazard	88
Long Way Home	89
Rest Stop	90
What If?	91
Tail End of Hope	92
Seismic Shifts	93
A Lesson in Roses	94
Restoration	95
Caution: Overload	96

Pulse of the Generations	97
The Truth About Troubles	98
Plea for Hope	99
Paid in Full	100
Trying	101
Lessons for My Child	102
Once Overwhelmed	103
Sudden Stillness	104
Digging Out	105
Day of Freedom	106
Small World	107
Tough Times	108
Wide Open Spaces	109
Soulful Mother	110
Room for You	111
Choices	112
Because You Are	113
Awake	114
Forgiveness, Step One	115
Priceless Gifts	116
Forget-Me-Not	117
Difficult Job	118
What's in It for Me?	119
Counting to Ten	120
Mind Games	121
Playtime	122
Day of Endless Failures	123
Response to Love	124
A Weighty Request	125
When Life Is Too Much	126
No More Stinkin' Thinkin'	127
Praise Song	128
Unloosed	129
Hearing Your Voice	130
Reflections	131

Everyday Miracles	132
Recognition of Beauty	133
Galpals	134
Coming to You in Prayer	135
Walk Away Gently	136
Inside/Outside	137
Self-Acceptance	138
Humility	139
Trust the Connections	140
Work It Out	141
Bless This Mess	142
Scared	143
Through Your Eyes	144
Your Presence Requested	145
Transparency	146
Seventh Day	147
You Know	148
Understanding 101	149
Finding Time	150
The Hike	151
Change Is Coming	152
Urban Dweller	153
Providence	154
This Garment	155
Paso Doble	156
After the Dark	157
Au Fait	158
Divine Moments	159
Stepping Back	160
Appoggiatura	161
Gifted	162
Friendly Aging	163
Rock Me Slowly	164
Standing Tall	165
Words Do Hurt	166

Let It Ring	167
The Gift	168
Women of All Faiths	169
Immeasurable Grace	170
Peace Plea	171
Three-Legged Stool	172
Broadcast	173
Touchstone	174
Job Over	175
Entrepreneur	176
Wisdom of Our Elders	177
This Amazing Soul	178
You, Everywhere	179
Apology	180
Knowing I Am Home	181
Daughter of the Woods	182
What Love Says	183
Making Way for Clarity	184
For All the Single Ladies	185
Priorities	186
You Are All	187
Muses	188
Child Inside Me	189
Danse Macabre	190
Listening	191
Rubber Meets Road	192
Thanks to You	193
The Reason	194
You, Me, and the Lamp Post	195
Sensing Grace	196
Office of Empathy	197
Just Desserts	198
Seek and You Will Find	199
Small Wonders	200

Introduction

A book of prayer must be many things to many people. Some open a prayer book and hope for the right words to carry them over to a place where they will be heard by the Divine. Others use it like they would a tool, as if they were pounding a nail with the perfect hammer. And still others hold it in their hands, close their eyes and create their own prayers. Women have shared with us their need for a new way to pray. They want short, contemporary prayers that tell their stories. The prayers you'll find in *Personal Peace: Prayers for Women of All Faiths* make it easier to have meaningful conversations with the Holy One. Lose yourself in the pages. Give it up to a higher power at the very same time as you turn inward. When you feel the weight of this prayer book in your hands, rest assured — you are not alone in your joy or your sorrow. You have one voice with all women of the many faiths that form our sisterhood.

Personal Peace: Prayers for Women of All Faiths is a collection of prayers written by women from different faith perspectives. Yet, with all the diversity these talented women writers represent, the message is the same: comfort, healing, joy, and peace. We ask for blessings of good health, security and happiness, and we are grateful for it, too. We pray with others in mind, we pray for our loved ones, and we pray for ourselves. Regardless of religion, nationality and social position, it always comes down to the three things we hold most dear — freedom from pain, worry and heartache.

The energy that inspires our authors comes from a movement disguised as a website. Prayables.com was born of the need to reach out to women and give them an easy way to add more prayer to their lives. We came together to write short, contemporary prayers that speak to the issues woman face today: Over-scheduling, financial worries, caring for our children and aging parents, or a difficult boss. These and more are themes you'll find in this prayer book. A Prayables-style prayer reads like poetry. It will touch your soul, because the words tell your story. Some stories make us laugh, and some make us cry. But all will leave you uplifted and closer to the Creator.

The world has opened up, and borders have expanded. Facebook, smart phones and ipads are just a few of the technologies that have rocked our world. There isn't an industry that is not affected by technology. Farmers in sub-Saharan Africa use cell phones to get the latest market prices for their harvest. Bearded rabbis, imams and priests have e-stores and preach from streaming video. When Prayables began, it was an online publisher of multi-faith prayers. We are now a social community of like-minded women who are tech-savvy and enjoy sharing a sacred space with "PrayPals" from different religions. But, even with all the gizmos and gadgets that we encounter every day, it's still about relationships.

Personal Peace: Prayers for Women of All Faiths is a relationship builder. The ultimate bond comes from the heart and leads to the soul.

I'm praying that in these pages, you will find insight, meaning, and connection to your own personal peace. It is said, if a woman is at peace, her family is at peace. If a family is at peace, their community is at peace. And when communities find peace, the world will find peace. Shalom.

- Susan Diamond, Prayables Publisher

A User's Guide to *Personal Peace: Prayers for Women of All Faiths*

Welcome to this book, women of all faiths. We are glad you are here. I imagine a user's guide to a book seems an odd concept: We all know how to use a book, right?

Yes, but we want *Personal Peace* to be more than just a book. We hope that it will be a guide, a personal companion. We've created our prayers to conform to any and all worship styles, but we want you to go further and truly make them yours. Tab the pages of prayers that give you comfort. Write in the margins. Change the words to suit your life situation. Feel free to add the name of your Higher Power to the prayers.

We've included a Table of Contents so you can scan for a prayer title that speaks to you. You can also simply dive in anywhere. Try holding a question or problem in your mind and opening the book at random. Sometimes the right words will find you.

Use the prayers as a starting point for meditation or reflection. Add one to your life every morning or evening, then spend some time thinking about how the words apply to your own life and sense of personal peace.

And don't forget to listen to your own inner voice: We've left blank pages at the end of the book, so you can write down your own special prayers.

What we hope, of course, is that you will leave your mark all over these pages. We hope it will be not just *a* book, but *your* book, a deeply personal source of perfect peace.

- Lori Strawn, Editor

Personal Peace

I praise You for:
My purpose,
My passion,
My partner,
My people,
My portable peace,

Your perfection experienced.

For purpose gives direction.
Passion unleashes my gifts.
My partner, life meaning.
My people, a heritage.
My portable peace is
Your grace unequaled.

- Ruth Williams

Radiant Morning!

What a wild burst of energy today!
I woke this morning
to Your beautiful sunlight,
to Your blue skies,
and a world of possibility!

I am motivated.
I am ready.
I am Yours.

Let's take this day together!
I will turn my back on past mistakes,
walking ahead
in the rays of Your brilliant light!

I am energized.
I am healthy.
My heart is full.

Thank You for this new day!
A new opportunity to pursue
everything that I am meant to be
and will be in You!

- Abigail Wurdeman

I Am the Diamond

I met them in a restaurant,
running late as usual.
Taking too long to look perfect.
Brand new outfit, hair just done.
Must give them the impression,
I've got it all together.

But I still won't measure up.
They who have better jobs,
bigger houses, smarter kids,
more loving husbands.
Feeling jealous, I tell lies.
Weaving them into truths until
I don't recognize the person I've become.

I implore You,
help me to see myself
through Your eyes.
Help me to know self-love,
self-worth, self-confidence.
So I no longer feel inadequate.

A complete creation of Your finest work,
I am the diamond, You are the jeweler.
Every facet of my being is exquisite.
We are all Your diamonds.
Different clarity, different cut,
and all perfect in Your eyes.

- Heidi Haller

Journey = Destination

Let me ask an unusual thing:
Bless the people
with their cranky pants on this morning.
The ones who got off
on the wrong foot today.
Who woke up
on the wrong side of the bed.
Show them that each moment
spawns another choice.
That there is no great abacus in the sky
meting out glitches.

Nudge them toward knowing you can always,
hitch up the sail and turn the ship's wheel,
and set course for the serene blue horizon.

Help me too, to keep in mind
it's their bad day, not mine.
Steer me toward my own crystal morn.

- Ruth Williams

Ritual

First, I will clear the space that surrounds us.
I set aside the clutter of my day
so the chaos does not obstruct my view of You.

Then, I will clear myself.
I breathe out the weight of my ego
so my heart is opened to you.

Then, I will open my eyes.
I find you at my side,
waiting for my frantic mind to settle finally on You.

Now we meet,
joined in the sacred ceremony of our routine,
in the quiet motions that tell my wild heart
it's time to be still . . .
in this moment I am with You
and nowhere else.

- Abigail Wurdeman

Light in the Depths

Down here
where only the lantern-fish swim,
too deep for sun to penetrate,
I see a glint.

It is You, reaching for me
through the churning seas,
a hand to pull me back to the surface
and into the light.

I had made myself a home here,
among the shipwrecks,
thinking I'd never return to the shore.
But You saved me,
hauled me heaving onto dry land,
blinded my eyes with illuminating love.

How do Your arms reach so very far?
I can only wonder at Your mercy.
You blow life into me;
I am lighter than air.

- Lori Strawn

Peacemakers

Blessed are those who
speak the words that calm us,
quiet us, and bring us back to you.
Blessed are those who,
with a look or a touch,
still the fear that leads to hate.

Oh, help me to be
one of your peacemakers.
Where there is strife,
help me bring calm.
Where there is pain,
help me bring healing.

As I go through my day
and make the world a better place,
help me reflect Your light, Your love,
and Your ever-present wisdom.

- Sue Bradford Edwards

Amazed

This is my day
of unlimited chances.
A day of uncommon favor
and unending blessings.

When Your favor
and blessings overtake me,
my change will come.
I am ready and prepared
to receive my portion.
It is my turn to prosper.

I don't fear today,
for fear tolerated
is favor unsure.

I experience Your goodness.
I have unleashed my faith
and I am amazed.

This is my day
of miracles
I receive it! I receive it!

- Brenda Scott

Whatever May Come

I'm getting the idea
you know what the heck You're doing.

You made me funny, fickle,
sometimes feral,
but You know I always
find my way back to center.

You gave me the quirks I possess,
like a penchant for pointless puns,
a black thumb unable to sustain even a ficus,
and a heart as wide as the sky.

Measuring myself against others who aren't me
is like saying I don't trust You.
My greatest idiosyncrasy
is that I've never met You,
but trust You with my life and all I hold dear.
Walk together with me, whatever may come.

- Ruth Williams

Don't Doubt It

Why this doubt?
Doubt in my work abilities,
in the appeal of my
body's plush form,
whether goodness will come
in tomorrow's sunrise.

Doubt whether I'm doing
all I should for my children,
whether I'm really the best
I can be for my partner.
Am I truly the best me?

Alleviate this doubt.
Help me trust in my work abilities,
in the beauty that is me,
that I am doing my best
for my children and my partner,
and goodness indeed shall come.

I trust You to help me deal with my doubt.
Refill my soul with confidence and love.
I know You will.
(I don't doubt it one bit.)

- Karen Laven

Promise of a New Day

Today I will work hard,
I will focus and endure.
And I will do so cheerfully,
because today I have the joy
of knowing I am "getting there."

I am grateful to You
for the work of the week,
and as I look at my to-do list,
I am grateful that there
is still time ahead
to complete unfinished tasks.

But my gratitude is great
for the relief that lies ahead,
for the knowledge that this work
is only one flavor of my life.

There will be time to balance,
to recharge and reconnect.
Thank You for the gift of that promise!

- Abigail Wurdeman

Prism of Compassion

If you knew the whole story,
you'd lead with love.

The lady who bumped you on the sidewalk?
She slept on the park bench last night.

The man who was rude in the restaurant?
He's waiting to hear
the results of his wife's biopsy.

One small kindness can make all the difference.

Please remind us:
You can't always tell from looking
what's weighing on a human heart.
Revive the humanity in us
as we bounce off each other in a crowded world.
Renew our spirits as we endure life's struggles.
Restore our souls when we feel we can't go on.

- Ruth Williams

My Last Pity Party

How did I get stuck doing this?
I fuss and fume
as I make the calls,
stuff the envelopes,
and line up the nametags.
I am slowly realizing
that just because
I *can* do something,
doesn't mean
I need to be the one
who says "yes."

Please help me see
that every job
is not destined to be mine.
Please help me understand
that I can say "no"
without being mean —
even when someone
is surprised
by my answer.

Give me the wisdom
to find a balance
between the many requests
that come my way
and the time and talents
You have given me.
As I find this balance,
help me rediscover
the joy I once felt
in sharing my talents with others.

- Sue Bradford Edwards

Silent Partner

Grace training began three years ago
with the first heartfelt prayer of my life:
Help me.
This isn't the life I would have chosen,
if I had my druthers.
As if I hadn't created my own life through years of
Settling For,
Making Do,
Getting By.
Thank You for this moment of clarity.
Every morning is a chance to start over.
My soul is worth nurturing, and this life is worth living.
Thank You, I have the whole world in front of me
and the entire universe behind me.

- Ruth Williams

A.M. & P.M.

This morning I wake and I thank You.
For the gift of seeing a new day begin,
and the energy I'll need, to make it through today.

When the day is over and nighttime comes,
I will thank You.
For the gift of knowing a day has been well-spent
and for the tranquility that comes with a darkened sky.
Morning to night, a precious cycle.
I am each day, grateful.

- Rachel Lee

Me Time

On my best days,
I know it isn't selfish
to make time for exercise —
to take time for me.
On dark days,
I doubt my choices.
Am I irresponsible,
neglecting my work,
family, and friends?

Help me realize
I deserve the nurturing
You provide for all of creation.
Caring for me is the first step
in caring for others.
I overcome the dark days
by embracing Your best days.

- Sue Bradford Edwards

Attention Shoppers

Why is it that what I want
is never on the rack?
Peace of mind.
Self-esteem.
Happiness.

I make myself believe
that a handbag will suffice,
but You know it never does.

Instead let's go shopping together,
You and I.
Only instead of shoes,
I'll look for hope,
purchase forgiveness,
pursue restraint.

For once, I'll leave with more
than I came in with.

- Lori Strawn

Give Me Shelter

My house still shelters us, but not for long.
Soon my family and I will be swept away
in the brutal tsunami that is foreclosure.
My house is no longer my house.

How do I get through this?
I need You to remind me,
my house is merely walls and nails.
My family's love always has a solid foundation.
That foundation can never be taken away.

- Karen Laven

Keeping Perspective

As always, my to-do list
is far too long,
with groceries to buy,
the house to clean,
and yard work to do.
Please help me keep
these tasks in perspective.
I'm in danger of reducing my life
to a daily check list.
Help me draw on your serenity,
so that I can remember
that we gather together
for more than food,
that no one is checking
to see if the house has been dusted.
With these things in mind,
I can focus on You,
and through You,
on those with whom
I share this special day.

- Sue Bradford Edwards

Intervention

The pain never stops.
It has become as much a part of me
as my skin, my eyes, my pulse.
Please, please intervene.

Reunite my body
with your blessings…
with joy and life and strength.
Remind me what it was to be safe in my body.
And when I cannot hear Your reminders,
cradle me close and rock me,
until the pain melts into the comfort of Your presence.

- Abigail Wurdeman

Hearth and Home

Please make me a better steward
of all those entrusted to my care.
Remind me that tending to those I love
is a high honor.
Help me to do my part
even when I feel wrung out
like the laundry on the line,
worn out like an old, weathered throw rug,
left behind like yesterday's newspaper.
Nobody's taking advantage
or taking me for granted.
I've chosen willingly to be there
for the ones in my life and my heart.
Bless me as I create a home
filled with loving-kindness
and let it permeate all souls who enter,
including my own.

- Ruth Williams

Grateful Start

Thank You for this day —
a fresh start,
a new opportunity,
a gift from You.

Thank You for filling it
with the joy of friends,
the wonder of what might be,
an awareness that You are here —
watching, waiting, loving,
more awesome than anything
that stands against me.

More loving than anyone
on this Earth.
More than I can imagine.
Thank You.

- Sue Bradford Edwards

Doubt

Be with me.
Not just in cloisters,
clouds and the parted sea.

Walk with me.
Reassure me that the
road is only unfamiliar
the first time I'm on it.

Speak to me concretely.
Take me past the metaphors
and middle men
and tell me why I doubt.

Reach out Your hand
to lift me back up
with Your grace
and complete me.

- Ruth Williams

Career Steps

I am at the very dawn of my career.
I know exactly where I want
this journey to lead.
You know, too;
time and again I have asked You
to take me there and now
I ask You once again.

I also ask that You grant me
wisdom in the journey.
Teach me to embrace each challenge
as a new lesson learned.
Help me recognize the joy of the work,
the unexpected truth
that there is as much delight
in the process as there is in the result.

Open my eyes that I might recognize my work
as a service to those around me,
teach me to cherish my career
for the good it enables me to do.

And when I have at last reached my goal,
remind me that I did so with You at my side,
so that I may offer you my gratitude
not only for what I have accomplished through You,
but also for who I have become.

- Abigail Wurdeman

Faith

The other day I had a thought.
The kind that weaves itself
into your mind and takes hold.

I realized that I am
constantly in fear.
Afraid that I won't be able to
meet the needs of those I love,
afraid that I'm not here for me.

You are my endless
source of possibilities.
Take me to Your place of calm,
and let me rest.

Fear cannot exist
side by side with faith.
Fill my thoughts with
the certainty that my faith in You
is stronger than my faith in fear.

- Heidi Haller

Morning

I spend the day alone with my thoughts.
They're spread among endless coffee cups,
strewn between papers that need grading.
They taunt me like books stacked on my floor,
ones that need to be read and resolved.

Help me to remember amidst this scurry:
Every morning we have the choice
to race through this busy life,
or sit still, feel You and learn
to pray again for the first time.

- Miranda Claudius

One Soft and Certain Voice

I feel as though I am at
everyone's beck and call.
I am surrounded
by a chorus of needs
and I cannot hear myself anymore.
I cannot hear You.

I want to give to my family,
to my friends, to my coworkers.
But there is only so much of me.
Please burst through the crowd.
Quiet the cacophony.
Make Your voice the only one I hear.

Show me the needs of my loved ones
and tell me how to help.
Show me my own needs
and teach me how to protect them.
Show me how to support my friends and family
without always saying "yes."

And when I lie down at the end of the day,
please bring me the satisfaction of knowing
I had a day of good choices,
enabling me to come closer to being the woman I want to be
for myself, for my loved ones, and for You.

- Abigail Wurdeman

Army of Hope

In a world rocked by devastation,
by earthquakes and tsunamis,
by starvation and cruelty,
I am only one person.

It is so easy to claim I can do nothing,
so easy to be intimidated
by the disasters before me.

Please soften my heart again.
Remind me of my brothers and sisters,
of all your servants, standing together,
each of us filling just one belly,
buying just one school book,
building just one house.

Grant me a willing heart,
that I may join your army of hope,
trusting that the work of Your hands
will make significant the work of mine.

- Abigail Wurdeman

Tearing Down the Anger

I did it again. I yelled.
After I promised You I would learn control,
my anger took hold, escaped.
I made them cry.
Me who loves them more than life itself.
How could I do that?
You need to help me here
or I will undo the few things I have done right.

Please guide me to be a person
who speaks words that build, not tear down.
May your love and goodness fill my heart and my mouth.
When I speak, bring forth Your words of esteem and life.
Let me give to others, Your unconditional love,
For I am shaped in Your image.

- Heidi Haller

Energy Rush

Today is a day for living!
I step into sunlight, blinking,
unused to bona fide illumination.
What wonders You have laid before me!
Let us drink them in together.

Today is a shot of Vitamin C.
I thank You for its energy, its pulse;
for bringing me back — wham! whoosh! —
into the thick of the heart of action,
all the living that lies outside my head,
beyond my front door.

Open me up to the whole wide world.
Let me experience You
in smell, sound, sight, touch, taste.
Involve me in Your creation.
I cannot wait to spend the day with You.

- Lori Strawn

Unfolding

I belong to You.
I know this best when I am here,
sharing this space and time
with only You, with exactly You.

I unfold here,
bringing each part of myself forward again
to be seen by Your familiar eyes
and to be held
in Your focused affection.

Please unfold for me, too.
Let me meet You the way You meet me —
with exclusive attention,
with specific love,
with deliberate commitment.

And should I find distraction in a dozen other voices,
I pray You draw me in again,
back to the perfect home of Your presence.

- Abigail Wurdeman

Faith Vs. Reason

I'm here,
You're there,
And yet, we're together.

I've been around the block, around the world.
Somehow, You're everywhere I go.

Make me mindful that life is not all or nothing.

Embolden me as I fail forward
Knowing that the only mistake would be not to try.

Inspire me to progress every single day.

Remind me not to take it personally
When I call and You don't pick up.

You gave me the gift of reason
Precisely so I would ask questions.
Be patient with me as I engage my senses
And still find the faith to follow my heart.

- Ruth Williams

Shout

I shout out for triumph,
I shout out for love,
I shout out for happiness,
my sickness has been healed!

You hear my victory,
You hear my devotion,
You hear my joy,
my prayers are answered!

- Brenda Scott

Sacred Agent

I ask that you make me Yours —
not only your child,
your wayward lamb —
but also Your instrument,
your agent of change.

Teach me to surrender not to the darkness,
but to the light of possibility,
as Your strength sustains me
and Your wisdom guides me.

For once, I will not shrink into the fear of insufficiency;
I will stand and face the darkness,
assured of your support,
praising You for this blessed duty.

- Abigail Wurdeman

Lost and Found

I've done it again.
I'd lose my own head if it wasn't attached.
Please.
It seems like such a little thing.
But I could use:
Your eyes, to see the unseen,
Your attentiveness,
so as not to repeat the fault,
Your forgiveness, for being so careless
with the many gifts you give me.
Help me recover what has been lost.
You, who I can never lose,
no matter how forgetful I become.

- Lori Strawn

What Happened?

I was asked for a favor.
I loaned the money:
to pay bills, to pay rent,
to buy food for the children.

She promised to pay me back.
Next week turns into next year.
The phone calls stop.
Our short conversations
of friendship are gone.
A need fulfilled
turns into friendship's end.
What happened?

Help me to hear Your voice
reassuring me I did the right thing.
Helping someone in need, being a good friend
and being willing to do it all over again.

- Brenda Scott

Listening for You

Time and time again,
I bring my concerns and worries to You.
But when I try to hear Your voice,
something always gets in the way.
The phone rings.
The oven timer goes off.
Someone calls my name.
Please help me find a time,
a place, a way to hear
what it is You need to tell me.
I know You will speak to me.
I simply need Your help
to find the space and the quiet to hear
what You have to say.

- Sue Bradford Edwards

Sailing Forth

Today I am at sea,
yet not far from the harbor.
I row forward, scenting progress,
yet prone to doubt my own abilities.
Dearest Companion,
help me experience this day
like Balboa, first sighting the Pacific:
wide-eyed, without cynicism,
a vista of incredible opportunities,
with endless routes to success.
Please stay close by;
this ship takes two to steer.

- Lori Strawn

Simple Sign

Tonight, I am full
of uncertainties:
rushing water, rocks
and loosened stones.
Above me, stars reach
connecting pieces of
my scattered life, forming
constellations of doubt.

But when all is quiet,
I hear the creek
pulsing outside my window.
Your presence is there.
It is pushing, persevering
through broken waters,
even after a day of storm.

I may never know what will be.
But tonight I know for sure
that You are ever near.
I believe everything keeps moving.

- Miranda Claudius

Impossibly Alive

I was absolutely certain
I was going to die.
I saw the world spin around me
while my hands gripped the wheel
and my foot frantically pumped the break.
I pled with You; I begged for my life.

And You were beside me.
Taking control because I could not.
Your strong hands guided me to safety
and Your soft voice quieted my wild mind.
Now, remembering my hands trembling
and a voice unsteady
I offer You my humble thanks
for honoring my life by saving it.

- Abigail Wurdeman

Name Changing

Looked at the pile of bills
and decided to adjust my glasses.
Must be a great new job
coming to cover it all.

Looked at the bottles of pills
to fix my health woes
and re-set my compass.
Must be miracle coming in my body
to make me whole again.

Looked at the wars in the world
and opened my mind and heart
as wide as they would go.
Must be ambassadors of peace
coming to every village and people.

Looked at each thing I saw
as a problem and
gave it a new name: whoppertunity.
It's a hell of a big pile of trouble,
but we've got You on our side.

- Ruth Williams

Next Opportunity

Discouragement covers me
like piles of papers on this desk.
The light in my job is gone.
I dream often of leaving
the struggles of dreary days
and finding a new start.

But I know too well:
I'm too practical to quit,
too lazy to leave,
too ashamed to walk away,
again.

Somewhere I have stored
the confidence I need.
Someday I know
a better job awaits.
Somehow I believe
You will show me:
that bright and
ready path of change.

- Rachel Lee

Ever-Present

I lost my nerve today
and You led me back to it.
What would I do without Your
ever-present support?

Thank You for never,
tiring
tiring
tiring of my repetitive
pleas and failings.

You are:
ever-patient
ever-forgiving
ever-loving.

I am merely:
ever-human
ever-sinful
ever-grateful for You.

- Karen Laven

A Marriage in Trouble

We sit in silence.
I say nothing;
he looks at the TV
while I stroke the cat.
The couch is small,
but miles separate us.

A stranger in my home.
I rub my arm,
desperately needing
to feel touch.
Please can't You heal
this pain, his heart,
my contempt, his indifference?

Give me the courage
to break down the barriers,
learn the truth,
repair the damage,
to rebuild.

I lift up this relationship
to You to bless.
Give me discernment and strength
to separate myself from the past.
I release this burden to You,
the architect of my future.

- Heidi Haller

Granddaughter

I am overwhelmed with gratitude to You
for putting this child of my child
onto this earth and into my life.

Her presence has brought me a joy
I'd never known, an abundant joy,
ever-bubbling; a transcendental bliss.

I thank You for this miracle,
for the chance to hold her,
and to cherish her.
To love her with a ferocity
that can only hail from You.

- Karen Laven

Trying Times

I don't know where, I don't know when,
but something's got to give.
I'm just gonna talk turkey (even though it's not Thanksgiving).
Gonna lay my cards on the table (even though we're not in Vegas).
You've really been putting me through it.

Sent me up that creek without a paddle.
But I'm not giving up on You.
I'm too stubborn for that.
All that I've been through, all the answers I still don't have.
It all comes down to this: I don't know how, but I know Who.
Shore me up until I can stand on my own again.

- Ruth Williams

Raging Heart

I feel my anger overpowering me.
I have lost my sense of balance
my sense of control
my sense of security.
Now I stumble my way to You and ask You,
lay a calming hand over my raging heart.

Give me the wisdom to see my righteous anger
as an alert to danger,
so that I can respond by caring for myself.

Help me resist the desire to treat my anger as a weapon,
so that I will not perpetuate hurt
by responding with aggression.

And please teach me grace,
so that I may know peace by learning to forgive.

- Abigail Wurdeman

With Me

Here beside You, I am known.
You have the words I cannot find.
You know the truths I will not speak.
You offer me peace I thought was out of reach.
You are my warmest companion, my perfect joy.

- Abigail Wurdeman

Sick and Tired

The aches still ache.
The pain hasn't gone away.
I'm sick of myself.
Tired of being focused
day and night on how I hurt.
On what I cannot do,
and what the next test
might show or cost.

Help me look beyond myself.
Teach me to realize
that no one woman
can live with pain, alone.
Share Your:
Compassion,
Love,
Patience.
And I will concentrate on
wellness today and tomorrow
with You by my side.

- Sue Bradford Edwards

Open Soul Surgery

You gave me the
expanse of eternity
as my birthright,
this space that I inhabit
tentatively and
always so circumspect.

You created galaxies,
rain forests and archipelagos
to illustrate what is possible.
Yet, sometimes all I see
is my small subdivision
of space and time.
Remind me, I asked to be
eternal,
embraced,
exponential.

Please turn on that one
specific star I see
each winter night.
The one burning
against a black sea.

Give me Your vision so
it will be finally clear to me.
I'm not alone on the journey
and the road is blissfully
never-ending.

- Ruth Williams

Miracles of Routine

I wake.
I am blessed to meet the new day.
I stretch and snuggle;
I am blessed with arms,
legs and body at my command.
I open my eyes;
I am blessed with vision.

I listen to the sounds
and silence around me;
I am blessed with hearing.

I get out of bed;
I am blessed with the ability
to stand tall and walk.
I enter the bathroom;
I am blessed to rid my body of waste.

I dress;
I am blessed to be protected
from the elements.
I'm ready to share
myself with the world;
I am blessed to recognize
these everyday miracles.

- Rachel Lee

Erasure

It feels like this one more interview
might just be it.
I declare an opportunity
to come in my life.
Right Now!

I am not too old; I am not too young.
I will learn new skills because
I want this job!

Erase old thoughts of "not good enough."
Replace in me a new acceptance of myself.
Lead me to better employment.
I trust in You!

- Brenda Scott

Forgive, Forget, Move On

How can I ever forget?
You tell me forgiving begets forgetting.
Easier said than done.
I nurse my hurts and keep them close,
like treasured souvenirs.
Pry open my fists and force them loose.
It is time to move on,
even though I'm afraid of the road ahead,
what it looks like
without the distraction of old wounds.
You will have to push me.
You will have to help me see without distrust,
as a newborn sees.
The world is going to look different.
I am ready to envision it.

- Lori Strawn

M-Word

I have been afraid of money . . .
afraid that understanding finances
would make me cold,
that preferring security
makes me faithless,
that wishing for prosperity
makes me greedy.

Please clear my heart of fear,
so that You can finally provide for me
by teaching me to provide for myself.

Grant me the courage to put a price on my work,
the wisdom to govern my finances,
the peace of mind to enjoy prosperity without guilt.

And as You teach me self-sufficiency,
please keep my priorities in check,
that I may spend what I earn in a way that honors
myself, my world, and You.

- Abigail Wurdeman

Soul of Philanthropy

You have placed within me my soul.
It gives form to my thoughts, creating
my innermost feelings
and driving my actions.
I am possessed with goodness
and remarkable power.
Committed to: doing deeds
of loving kindness,
speaking out for justice,
sharing my money with those in need.
I am one of this magnificent movement
to repair the world.

- Rachel Lee

One Hot Mama

I am SO hot.
Not hot like Megan Fox hot.
Hot like Bea Arthur in a raging sauna hot.
30 degrees outside, 65 degrees inside.
I sit, in short sleeves, waving a fan
crafted from today's junk mail,
discretely slipping ice down the front of my shirt.

I see You have a sense of humor.
It is hell getting old.
The heat and inner flames
come right along with it.

Could You help me cope with these
sudden interior flashes of 250 degrees?
I've been cast as the
Wicked Witch of the West,
without any fancy byline.
I am meltiiiiiiing…

I trust You to help me navigate
these hot springs of my life.
Transport me to my next stage,
where I will prosper and grow,
with your guidance and love.
I trust You to get me through.
Yes, this hot flash —
and all the others — shall pass.

- Karen Laven

Climbing Mountains

Today is my most dreaded day.
It is a day for beginnings —
and beginnings are hard.
I crane my neck to survey the day.
The sheer face of it looks insurmountable.
Take my hand and guide me over this day.
Teach me not to fear it,
but to embrace its possibilities.
Show me that each day
is an opportunity for change, reinvention.
Will You help me take a fresh approach,
a bold, new step in a different direction?
Thank You for the challenge,
and for Your hand to hold as I set out on
the untracked path of a new beginning.

- Lori Strawn

Waiters

I wait and I wish.
I don't want to be a waiter,
always getting ready
but never going forth.
I don't want to keep wishing,
dreaming of action
but frozen in place.
I have so many things
I want to do in my life.

I am sending out positive vibes,
waiting and wishing for You.
Teach me how to go for it,
how to be assertive.

Push me into the paths of people
who will work with me.
Help me to do all that I can to
reap the harvest You have in store for me.
I'm ready. I'm not just waiting any longer.

- Brenda Scott

Moving Mountains

You see what I am up against.
My head is bloodied from banging it against
the wall of corruption and denial.
Save me.

I am shadow boxing, trying to make a change,
yet all I strike is empty air.
Give me strength to keep fighting.

Let the justice of my cause break down the walls.
You, who alone have power over the powers-that-be,
let righteousness be done, in my name, and in Yours.

- Lori Strawn

Wrapping Up

Each day is a gift;
and now I tie the ribbon —
wrapping up work, looking forward to rest.
Thank You for the thousand ways
You have lent a hand to me.
Through every meeting and every interaction,
through every dirty face and unwashed dish,
You have been my guide.
Help me end each day as I seek to begin it:
with hope, strength, patience, and peace.

- Lori Strawn

Soul Mate

I search for your face
wherever I go.
What do you look like?
Surely, when our eyes meet
there will be this instant
spark of recognition,
allowing our destinies
to collide.

Almost everyone I know
has found their half-moon.
When placed together
they form one perfect heart.
Where is my soul mate,
the one You have chosen
just for me?

Can You see how
lonely I am?
Do You see how
I ache with emptiness?
Will You bring him now
to comfort me, love me,
complete me?

You, who has the power
to hear my prayers
and answer them;
You, who has the grace
to fill me with hope
please shower me
with Your compassion.

Let tomorrow be the day
Your divine intervention
brings us to our future.

- Heidi Haller

Rendering

I come to pray, but sit in silence.
I am listening for You to talk to me.
You whisper:

Come, let go your heavy burdens.
Raise up your weary arms,
all the light and yearning they hold.
Into my hands, rest your hunger and hurt.
Believe all you seek is not beyond hope.
Trust it is not outside your being.

- Miranda Claudius

Devastation

So many faces from other nations
coming to offer their help.
Mothers, sisters, aunts,
fathers, brothers, uncles,
cousins, nieces, nephews,
children are all gone.

Little things are reasons to be grateful:
comfort, a smile, hugs, tears.
The devastation makes us hurt;
it is not for us to question why.
We know You have made a way
for the hunger and the pain
to ease through others
giving their money, time, prayers —
Your will be done!

- Brenda Scott

Question

Why does everything happen to me?
What do I do when I don't know what to do?

How much more can I take?
What do I do when I don't know what to do?

When will it end?
What do I do when I don't know what to do?

I give it to You, to intercede for my good.
I love You!
I worship You!
I adore You!
I do all this…I know what to do.

- Brenda Scott

Until

Expectation seems to define my life.
I watch as kettles boil and clocks click midnight.
Calendars turn and leaves fall to the ground.
Still I linger, seeking some quiet secret.
I hang on, believing in Your goodness.

I know waiting is the hardest of hardships.
It's a thawing of icicles, the sluggish drip
outside my winter window announcing,
slowly, that spring will surely come.
Give me the courage to wait for tomorrow.

- Miranda Claudius

Rebirth

Today I am born.
I thank You for the view from here,
for the wide, unworn road
stretching out before me,
for all the possibility
simmering beneath the surfaces
of appointments and deadlines.

Thank You for standing
beside me today,
stepping with me into
another new beginning
and filling me with
the insuppressible joy
of Your constant presence.

- Abigail Wurdeman

Make Life, Make Sense

Woke up and felt a fissure
in my faith today,
but there is just no way
to take my heart out of its groove.

All is well.
There's always a way.
Help me get past
my need for everything
to make sense right now.

Abide with me.
Tolerate my lapses.
I'll take the trials,
if they come with a home
filled with warmth and laughter.

I'll bear up under the pain
if it leads to a deeper faith.
I can't see the whole tapestry;
help me not to pull
a stray thread in anger,
unraveling myself in the process.

- Ruth Williams

Divine Timing

I am so impatient,
sighing and stomping around my room.
I've been praying for a full year now.

Do You give points for faithfulness?
My numbers surely must impress.

What can I do to rush Your answer:
Light a candle?
Or should I fast?

Would you please give me a sign?
Nothing big, I'll know it's You.

OK — new prayer.
I get it.
"You who supplies my every breath,
I beg You — teach me patience,
help me recognize a prayer answered."

You hear me.
I'll wait and watch.
Your timing is always perfect.

- Heidi Haller

Sisters by Choice

She's the one I turn to in
moments of sheer panic.
A straight shooter who tells it like it is.
She's the cavalry rushing in,
saving me from myself,
talking me down from the ledge.
She's the one responsible
for uncontrollable
bursts of laughter,
playing off each other
until our mascara runs.
She's my touchstone, the one friend
I could never live without.

Thank You for her incredible gift of empathy,
always knowing my feelings.
Thank You for her quick mind;
she really gets me.
Thank You for her all encompassing love,
that never knows boundaries.
Thank You for making us sisters by choice
and my very best friend.

- Heidi Haller

Only Child

"Help me."
I seem to say that a lot.
You must be tired of my constant pleas.
Yet You remain as close as my shadow
as constant as breathing.
You spoil me with your constancy.
How good of You to favor each one of us
as though we are an only child,
Your ear tuned to the particular pitch
of each of our cries.
Mother, Father, Friend:
Thank You for listening.

- Lori Strawn

You Are There

I pause in washing the dishes,
answering email,
picking up the mess of an average day.
I wish I could feel You
here
with me.
Help me to realize that
You are there even when I cannot sense You,
that You are the constant in my life.
Where I am today,
there You are.
Where I am tomorrow,
You will be —
mountain, desert, or seaside,
apartment, house or condo.
You are there
waiting for me to look up,
to look out, and see.

- Sue Bradford Edwards

Music Within

I want my life to ring,
to surge like a cello,
deep and moving
graceful and resonant —
the sound of Your voice
when you speak to me.

I hear little songs
in my mind
of Your promises.
They carry me
through each day,
and I dance.

- Miranda Claudius

Perfect Victim

He saw from the first that I was perfect.
I did not scream.
I hid his ugly secret under layers of pain
deep in my soul. I told no one.
No one, that is, but You.
Please help me learn how to trust again.

Help me to stop seeing his face
on those that hold no blame.
Tell me, over and over,
that it was not my fault.

I pray for those he might have harmed
because I held my tongue.
Forgive me.
This wound is so deep,
only You can heal it.

Touch my heart. Make me well:
Master of myself, no longer victim.

- Lori Strawn

Abiding

I see a pile of bills
and I ask You:
Open the floodgates of increase
and help me find a way.

I see the medicine bottles on my counter
and I ask You:
Rain down favor on me
to make me whole again.

I see wars around me
and I ask You:
Open the minds and hearts
of the leaders of the world so
they may be ambassadors
of peace to their people.

- Ruth Williams

Arms Around Me

I thought I knew this person,
but I have not loved wisely.
The relationship is ending;
it was toxic for us both.

Teach me to move on
without bitterness and regret.
Help me to forgive myself
while I seek a better other.

Let me feel Your spiritual arms
supporting me as I weep.
Let me gain from You the certainty:
This decision is good,
and sits well in my soul.

- Brenda Scott

Measure of Success

Help me to recalibrate
so that I don't live by
everyone else's rules:
It's impossible to achieve success later in life.
You're a woman in a man's world.
Change is something to be feared.

Help me to regroup so that
those who populate my world
are kindred spirits
with the best intentions.

Help me to refocus
so that I remember
who I am
and whose I am.

If You are with me,
there is nothing
else to prove.

- Ruth Williams

Off the Shelf

My faith is too delicate
to even speak some days.
It is a flower, a vase, a glass
that I fear doubt can break.

But I shall not leave it
on a shelf collecting dust.
I shall not place it out of reach —
something I see, but never use.

So fill me, over and over,
with peace.
Help me to believe in Your
constant, unceasing strength.

- Miranda Claudius

Fussing Over the Folks

Help me to not worry
when the phone rings and rings
and my messages go unanswered.
Let me take a deep breath
and picture them:
not in a ditch,
but where they usually are these days —
touring a winery,
hiking a woodland path,
or on yet another trip.

The life they are living today is
their reward for years of labor,
sacrifices made when we were children.
I know this even as I envy them.

They have the leisure I want for myself.
But today, it is theirs.
Let my smile mirror your smile,
as they enjoy their health,
their time, and their lives,
dedicated at long last to enjoying the world
You have made and the leisure You grant.

- Sue Bradford Edwards

Living Fully

I feel helpless today.
I feel that everything I want is impossible.
I am bound to suffer.
If I trust You to provide me
with all that I need to live fully —
will a miracle happen?
I let go.
Today, I make way for miracles.

- Robyn Cruze

Inertia

It's so hard to get motivated
to change the things I can.
I tell myself I must let go
of what does not nourish me.
I shouldn't just live
with "the devil I know."

There is a lioness in me
that needs to roar
and a great, golden path
that leads to peace.
I ask You, discombobulate me,
shake my boots, and I know
I will be so much more.
Miracles accrue,
one prayer at a time.

- Ruth Williams

Momentum

Today, it is full speed ahead.
Here I stand
with my focus on the road ahead
and Your powerful hand
against my back,
pressing me ever forward
toward a life well-spent.

Thank You for the potential
that remains in each day,
and for the energetic spirit
You bestow, so that I may
encounter life's challenges —
its failures and victories —
with a nimble and sturdy heart.

- Abigail Wurdeman

I Am Ageless

What if there were no mirrors
upon which to reflect?
Would I strive harder, laugh louder,
believe in myself more?
Would I embrace a world filled with
endless possibilities?

What if birthdays had no numbers,
just a celebration of this life?
I fear growing older.
Will You help me with my struggle?
Can You bring forward this child
trapped in another's skin?

You, who knows my song,
You, who can give it wings,
please, tomorrow let me wake up
not feeling scared,
knowing that with You, I am renewed.
I am young; I am eternal.
I am forever ageless.

- Heidi Haller

Road Map

Today I feel lost,
so I turn to You for direction.
My heart is a compass.
Set me to true north.
Lead me where I need to go.

Be my guide.
Take me with you,
for you know the roads.
I know the climb will be arduous.
But when I get there,
oh, the view will be worth it!

- Lori Strawn

Finding Home

I wish for a house
with many rooms
to hold all my prayers
for you, my friend.

Happiness will sleep
in the still places:
in cups of tea, picture frames
and the smell of hope
that wraps around walls.

- Miranda Claudius

Free at Last!

I quit judging, fudging, procrastinating,
gossiping, belittling —
my personal pity party.

I forgive my partner, my relatives,
my friends, my workmates and boss,
myself.

I embrace kindness,
empathy, benevolence,
those who need me most,
You.

- Karen Laven

Stuck In My Head

Worries and fears
swirl through my mind,
keeping me tense,
unrested and unwell.
Help me to replace
this darkness
with lightness and hope,
joy and well-being.
Help me to learn
to draw what comes
from You
into my center,
replacing what has no place there.
Fill me with what is good
so that I can reflect all
that You give me
back into the world.

- Sue Bradford Edwards

Reaching Up and Out

When I feel that I cannot truly help,
please help me reach up to You.
Lend me Your strength
so that I can see
that although I cannot fix
the problem itself,
there are a hundred other things
that I can do
that will bring comfort
that will show love
that will bring a hint
of You into her day.
Please help me reach up to You,
so that I may reach out in love.

- Sue Bradford Edwards

Workplace Hazard

I dread the workday.
Every day I struggle to keep peace
with a difficult coworker.
When I work with this person
I feel my sense of self-worth diminish.
I feel disrespected and unheard.
As I go into work,
I feel myself bracing for a blow.

Please surround me today
with Your perfect peace.
Help me react to the blows as they come,
rather than agonizing in anticipation of them.
Give me the strength to stand up
for myself when it is called for,
the patience to work peacefully
with someone I do not agree with,
and the joy to be a positive presence,
regardless of the challenges I confront.

- Abigail Wurdeman

Long Way Home

I heard the call many moons ago,
but turned away to "find myself."
Thank You for going to all this trouble,
to sculpt me in skin and sinew,
to wait patiently as I came back into the fold.
You took me the long way home,
so I could reach my own conclusions.
Let me be all I can,
and thank You with my life.
Please, today and every day,
be in my heart as I find my way.

- Ruth Williams

Rest Stop

Today is the day for not doing.
A day for saying no
to the buzz and whir of daily life.
It is a day for savoring minutes.
Thank You for this day of rest.
Let Your peace descend on me,
like twilight falling.
Show me the joy of perfect quietude,
of listening to You in stillness.
Let the world stop,
if only for a moment,
so that I might treasure
what is beyond it: You,
who give me blessed work,
but also blessed rest.

- Lori Strawn

What If?

You probably think I should be over this by now.
A lifetime of temptation, giving up, starting again —
follow me into the turmoil of my mind.

My body will never be what I want it to be.
It's too late for my version of perfect.
Age eliminates firm arms, slender waist.

Truth broadcasts itself through my conscience.
What is left? Can I set new goals?
Eliminate old thought patterns?

What if I aim not for a perfect body, but a loving heart?
What if I learn to care about me, like You do?
What if I see myself as You see me?

Precious, beloved, created for joy.
I am important in my speck of the world.
I am grateful for your patience with me.
I begin again.

- Brenda Scott

Tail End of Hope

I cannot see the light
at the end anymore.
All I can see are the months
stretched out before me,
each one representing a new set of bills
I cannot pay.
I see no way out.
All I see is deeper debt,
deeper failure.
I would love for You to guide me out of this.
I am asking to be rescued.
I am asking to see results.

If this is not something You can give me right now,
please teach me patience.
Grant me the faith to hope for better times
and to believe in a worthwhile lesson learned.

Open my eyes to the many blessings that surround me now,
the blessings that I do not have the strength
or energy to search for myself.

And above all,
please show me Yourself,
so that in moments of greatest self-doubt,
I can find my way into your waiting arms
where I can understand that I am not in this alone.

- Abigail Wurdeman

Seismic Shifts

I believe in magic and miracles.
I believe that You said it, and that settles it.
Everything comes to me at just the right time,
in symmetry, in synchronicity, in Your time.

I await You in perfect repose.
There is nothing more that needs to be done.
No furious flailing, no sackcloth and ashes.

I remember my prayer — not even a year ago:
"Make me stronger."
You revealed to me the unerring equation:
Hardship + Prayer = Steel.

Help me to stand on my own two feet
and, at the same time, lean fully on You.

- Ruth Williams

A Lesson in Roses

I was thinking,
the other day,
about tea roses.
The splendid profusion
of hybrids —
two beautiful plants
bred together
into something
startlingly new
and impossibly lovely.

And it occurred to me
that it was something like a marriage:
The two of us,
starting out foreign to one another,
then growing together
into something
we never could have dreamed:
A perfect, blooming wonder.
And I realized:
You have been our sun,
feeding and warming us.
You have been our gardener,
tending and protecting us.
You have been our bioengineer,
bringing us together,
knowing we were better together
than alone.

I thank You
for this love
that is bigger than myself.
I thank you for my marriage,
this remarkable rose.

- Lori Strawn

Restoration

My body seems to have turned on me.
My head is fluid.
My stomach has flipped upside down
and I've got a wretched case
of the shivering sweats.

I am losing time to my sickness.
My body is an enemy.
Stay here with me, won't You?

Lay a cool hand on my forehead
and soothe my aching limbs.
Draw the fever out.
Warm what's chilled, cool what's heated.

Restore my health.
Restore my energy.
Restore my spirit.

Bring peace between my mind and my body,
so that each cares for the other,
supporting and sustaining.

Draw me into good health with a gracious heart,
to bring You praise
for the blessing of a healthy body.

- Abigail Wurdeman

Caution: Overload

I am poking my head above the paperwork
to cry out: Help! I am drowning!
Make no mistake,
I know I am blessed to be employed.
Sometimes I let it run my life,
when that's Your job.

I put this in Your hands.
Shrink it down to size,
so that I might weave it
into the fabric of my life,
just one part of a much bigger pattern —
One that glorifies You
and uplifts me in the process.

- Lori Strawn

Pulse of the Generations

We raise our faces to You.
You who has sustained countless generations
With the steadiness of Your love,
With the strength of Your wisdom.
You are the blood that unites us.
You are the pulse that revives us.
You are where we begin,
Where we end,
Where we are.

I look to You
With soul-bursting gratitude
For the blessing of family
And the gift of Your Presence
Within and around us.

- Abigail Wurdeman

The Truth about Troubles

If you just scan the headlines of my life, you'll think I'm delusional.
What in the world would make me think there's any hope?
Calloused hearts, empty stomachs, aimless souls.
Tail-gaters, back-stabbers, nay-sayers.

It seems that civility has become a casualty,
and that "human" is no longer the standard state of being.

Yet I know the truth about troubles.

It's the wind, the rain, the compost of life
that give rise to a blooming thing of beauty.

Sustain me through these times of trial.
From seedling to morning glory,
bursting from the ground, reaching toward the sun,
hope springs eternal.

- Ruth Williams

Plea for Hope

He stares unseeing into the distance.
He is so young;
his life full of possibilities —
but he can't feel it.
I fear I will say the wrong thing
and push him
beyond all hope, beyond all help.

Please help me reach out
with a steady hand.
Please help me speak in a calm voice.
I cannot heal him alone.
Help me find a place where others
can give him the help he needs.
Show him how to rediscover hope and life,
two gifts that come through You
each and every day.

- Abigail Wurdeman

Paid in Full

As the door to each source
of financial credit slowly
closes with a sickening click,
I pray You will help me
unclench the familiar
grip of fear invading
the pit of my stomach.

Help me remember to breathe.
Let me lift my eyes from the
pile of papers that have cast
their numerical reckoning
upon my weary spirit.

Help me to seek, instead,
the aching beauty of a sunset,
the mysterious hope of a full moon,
the cleansing comfort of gentle rain.

Help me trust that the Hand of Providence
will always hold the solution
to my troubling dilemmas.

- Sharon Sinclair

Trying

Help me to quit trying
to change things through worry.
Teach me to speak through You,
and my life will change automatically.
When I learn to change my thoughts,
my life-change will begin,
from the inside out.

I try so hard to have peace.
In the midst of my tribulation,
I declare Your love and power!

Help me to free myself from anxiety in my thought life.
I declare a fast from wrong thinking!

I feel life through my emotions,
I declare joy to come!

- Brenda Scott

Lessons For My Child

Help me to teach my child.
To give her wisdom
and show her how to choose
good people to be in her life.

Help me to teach my child
to look within
for her very best —
that You are her
strength and guidance.

Help me to teach her
that enemies will come
but through You she will
always be victorious.

Help me to teach my child
the blessings in doing for others.
Timing is everything!

- Brenda Scott

Once Overwhelmed

What if?
What then?
Tormenting thoughts
of random fears,
torrential rains
of worry pummeled
my sanctity to a flooded swamp
of muddy misery.

No more
what ifs,
what thens,
cascading through my
consciousness,
uncontrolled.

I seek You
when the raindrops start,
before the skies turn
bleakest black.
You steer me
through the fury into
the comforting warmth
of the horizon.

- Karen Laven

Sudden Stillness

Today I hold still
To balance and recharge,
To release the times before
And prepare for the times ahead.

With You here beside me,
My mind quiets to hear Your voice.
My heart opens to draw You in.
And, with Your peace
Within and around me,
I thank You for this opportunity
To be made new.

- Abigail Wurdeman

Digging Out

Dishes clutter the counters and sink.
Laundry mounds up beside the washer.
Junk mail, shoes, and more
cover every flat surface.
I can't get out from under it all.

I need family and friends around me,
but I'm ashamed of how I live.
Lend me the vision I need
to see one small task
I can accomplish each day.
Help me understand that things
did not get like this overnight.
Give me patience as progress
comes little by little.
Provide me the will and energy
for my chores, so that order comes
to my home in the same way You
bring blessings and beauty to my life.

- Sue Bradford Edwards

Day of Freedom

Thank You for this wild,
unfettered day!

This day may not be all play:
I still have chores to complete,
responsibilities to honor —
but the day is mine.
The schedule is in my hands.
Today, I choose my moments.

Thank You for this day to center myself,
to get caught up,
to refuel and blow off steam —
all in the order and
at the pace of my choosing.

Thank You for this day to remember
that I belong to myself
as much as I belong to anyone else.
Thank You for the incomparable honor
of belonging first and foremost to You.

- Abigail Wurdeman

Small World

Every time I run into a friend I haven't seen in decades,
she says, "small world."
But in truth, it's really quite large.
Big enough to accommodate you, me, whole countries,
small minds, shuttered hearts, hurtful habits.
Vivify us as we let the light inside fade out.
Resurrect the faith we may have lost.
Build us up again when we've crumbled to the core.
Walk beside my sister who doesn't believe.
Lead her not to the place of fervor but of quiet calm.
Comfort those who believe and those who don't,
as we share the sky, sea, earth and future.

- Ruth Williams

Tough Times

If I ever needed You before,
I surely need You right now.
It is too much pain for me to bear,
I can't make it without You.
Please hear my prayer:

Thank You for being my anchor,
nothing can move me today.
Thank You for making me sensitive,
I know it will be okay.
You are inside of me.
My spirit will be quiet and at peace.

- Brenda Scott

Wide Open Spaces

Everyone contains the breadth of eternity inside them.
Galaxies of possibility,
Dark matter, shooting stars.

We think we have no say in the matter,
That we are but specks on the continuum of time.

But every time we do the right thing
Even when nobody is looking,
Each time we "take it on faith,"
New worlds form and supernovas burst into being.

The horizon's wide open now; the past has been jettisoned.
Open my eyes to what is possible
And my heart to what's true.
Map out the uncharted skies for me so I know I'm on my way.

- Ruth Williams

Soulful Mother

Thank You for giving me the gift of life, my child,
the greatest human love I will ever know.
You are here with me,
always putting my child's needs first.
You are here with me,
duplicating my education, wisdom, and emotion.

It is Your will to leave life's prints
on the generations You give forth.
Forgiveness that comes naturally.
Seeking within for all answers.
Knowing that the universe respects a pure heart.

I am humbled by the experience of following my heart
in moments of joy and inspiration.
Thank You for giving me the gift of life, my child,
the importance of being called Mom.

- Brenda Scott

Room For You

In the tiny rooms
of this apartment,
I praise You.
Only through You
do I have shelter.
Only by your hand,
do I have laundry to do,
food to prepare, and
dishes to wash.
It may not be
a vast palace or
a mansion full of servants,
but it is where I am,
and I praise you
for all You have given me.

- Sue Bradford Edwards

Choices

I watch as he weighs the choices.
I want to tell him what to do.
"Make the safe choice."
"Make the choice that I want,
the one that keeps you close to me."
Help him to be more objective than I can be.

Help him to make the choice
that takes advantage of his strengths and his passions,
his knowledge and his abilities.
Help him to choose well.
Only You can give me the strength
to wait patiently until he decides.

Help me smile and congratulate him
in my heart and with my words,
as I see the man
You have helped him become.

- Sue Bradford Edwards

Because You Are

Right where I am is where I should be.
In the center of Your will,
the perfect place to rest and dream,
undisturbed.
When I need to go forth, You will tell me.
Your timing flawless, I will respond.
The path is not marked, but I don't worry;
soon Your way will be known.

I marvel.
There's no explanation or evidence of Your existence.
I know simply because You are as constant as the sun.
All the glory goes to You.
Sustaining me, shaping me, guarding me.
You, who gives me direction.

Blessed are we who know You.
May our many voices be pleasing to You.
May the many become all and the all become one.

- Heidi Haller

Awake

I can't sleep at night;
I can't bear feeling alone.
I don't know what I should do;
I feel so uneasy.

I have within me
a hunger to know You.
To know You in my mind,
my heart, my spirit, and my life.
I will find the way to worship You and
go to the depth of my soul, fully satisfied.

- Brenda Scott

Forgiveness, Step One

"You have to forgive him.
It's the right thing to do."

Why do they tell me to forgive and forget
when he beats me down with his words?
If I continue to live this life —
I will hate myself.

Please, lend me Your strength.
Let me lean on You as I walk away.
Lend me Your mercy, so that hate and fear
flow out of my heart and forgiveness will rush in.

Fill me with Your love and Your hope,
so that I will face tomorrow awash in Your grace.

- Sue Bradford Edwards

Priceless Gifts

I want to be the best mother I can be,
to honor my children
by providing boundaries.

Allow me to be in the moment with them,
soaking in all their love
and giving back with mine.

Create the will for my children
to come to me with their problems,
feeling safe, loved and cared for,
comforted by my presence.

Today, I will love, care and provide for myself;
only then can I give these priceless gifts away.

- Robyn Cruze

Forget-Me-Not

It's a knock at the door.
It's an invitation in the mail,
a nudge: "Call me."
And when I do,
such sweet relief.
Not a burden, but a bequest:
A bouquet of forget-me-nots,
disguised as pain.
I thank You for keeping me mindful
of that which is greater than me.
You in my sufferings,
in my struggles,
in my sorrow,
raise me higher
with every ache.

- Lori Strawn

Difficult Job

I will not expect
a pat on my back
for doing a good job.
I will go beyond
what people are expecting.
Every step I take
is an opportunity.
When others doubt me,
my faith will be my victory.

- Brenda Scott

What's in It for Me?

This whole experience
I'm growing through,
Your message I've received!
I must give more to those
I care for and love.

As a parent,
guide me to be more reassuring —
praising, giving hugs and kisses,
every day saying, "I love you."

As a wife,
let me be his refuge,
a partner that esteems
in moments of uncertainty.

As a daughter,
remind me more often
to talk to my parents —
not just when I should,
but because I want to hear their voices.

As a friend,
move me to do unexpected acts of kindness,
demonstrating how much I care.

As a co-worker,
inspire me to smile,
greeting everyone I pass today,
reaching out to the quiet one
who eats alone.

What's in it for me?
Everything.
Your love flowing through me
can change my world.

- Heidi Haller

Counting to Ten

My jaw clenches tight.
My shoulders draw up.
I snap and snarl at those around me.
Help me gather myself quietly together.

Make me aware of the calming breath
that I draw in,
as I count
slowly
to
ten.

Make me aware of the breath that flows out,
taking with it, tension and anxiety,
as I count
slowly
to
ten.

Help me calm my body and my soul
and to turn this calm
to each task that fills my day.
I will mindfully complete these tasks
in Your peaceful loving presence.

- Sue Bradford Edwards

Mind Games

Trigger my mind to love.
My thoughts will come alive.
I will love everyone
and everything today.
I am in control.
I can make the decision
to love today.
You have given me the gift of choice.
No matter what I am going through,
I will manifest the fruit of love.

- Brenda Scott

Playtime

Trees must be climbed,
pebbles thrown and puddles stomped.
Instead of calling him back,
help me share in the joy
of these sights, these sounds,
and these experiences.
Help me fight the urge
to look for the stain remover
until after we have had our fun,
run our race,
and laughed out loud.
With Your help,
I can relearn joy
in the sticky hands of a small
but gifted teacher,
as our laughter fills the days ahead.

- Sue Bradford Edwards

Day of Endless Failures

I feel as if I have not done
one single thing right today.
This day has been one failure
after another:
failures at work
failures at home
failures with friends.

I feel worthless and tired.
Incapable of being
the person I want to be.

And yet, You love me still.
My family, friends and coworkers
love me still.
Thank You for such unconditional love.

Tonight I ask you to help me
forgive myself
for the mistakes of the day,
and to wake me in the morning
with the beautiful realization that,
once again, You have made me new.

- Abigail Wurdeman

Response to Love

You are the center of everything.
You exist, I know.
You're there to keep me dreaming.
You ask me to keep trusting
in an infinite plan
that will surely bring peace.

So amid my sadness,
among this doubt,
to you, I say:
You are enough.
All this is enough.

I will. I will. I will. I will.

- Miranda Claudius

A Weighty Request

The needles sticks at a number
too high for my liking.
I just can't do this without You.
Please, help me today to avoid temptation.
Help me to eat mindfully,
to approach activity with enthusiasm,
to remember what I'm doing is a blessing,
not a punishment.
You, who makes all things possible,
make possible the potential
I seek for myself.
May I live up to Your vision.

- Lori Strawn

When Life Is Too Much

I am so tired.
Help me to get past my thoughts of
"What else can happen?"

It seems like every time I turn around,
the telephone rings with unwanted news.
Or, someone on the job is making demands,
and it's something I can't deliver.
I feel the best I can do is get by.

Yet it's not all about
just going through the motions.
I know, through You,
I always find a better way.
With exhaustion — I honor You.
With anxiety — I adore You.
With stress — I praise You.
I am refreshed.

- Brenda Scott

No More Stinkin' Thinkin'

My son's balled-up socks stink.
The litter box stinks.
Our poodle's breath stinks.

My attitude stinks.
My life stinks.
I need your guidance even more
when everything stinks.

Help me see beyond
the daily grind
of my household chores and lousy job
into the goodness of life.

- Karen Laven

Praise Song

Praise to You
who whispers to us
in a spring breeze,
in the sigh of leaves overhead,
in the chuckle of a running stream.

Praise to You
who cries out to us
in the roar of waves
endless,
ever present,
all encompassing,
making You known.

Praise to You
who calls to us
in the pop and creak of ice,
in the thump of snow sliding
in the stillness of a frozen day.

Praise to You
who puts Your song
in the hearts of the birds
and in all who gather
to sing to You.
Praise to You.

- Sue Bradford Edwards

Unloosed

Help me release.
Lay Your hands over my fists,
teach my fingers to relax,
to uncurl and spread wide,
letting my resentment fall away,
And leaving my palms open to receive
Your waiting blessings.

- Abigail Wurdeman

Hearing Your Voice

You know I don't always hear You,
when the task is difficult,
the journey hard,
the way ahead frightening.
Help me recognize the messengers
You send my way
even as You help me
find the courage
to carry out Your plans.

- Sue Bradford Edwards

Reflections

I look in the mirror and see a jumble of flaws.
Please, help me see myself as You see me:
Perfect. Whole. Capable.
Help me to view my defects as potential,
my awkwardness as a different beauty.
Prevent me from self-harm,
and from habits that bring me shame.
Help me to accept myself as I am,
just as You do,
with limitless kindness and forgiveness.

- Lori Strawn

Everyday Miracles

There are things
I don't understand,
but I count on them.
Electricity.
A compass.
Faith.

Things that light my way
and take me where I need to be.
Gravity.
Common sense.
You.

Things I count on to
keep my feet on the ground.
Melody.
Tenacity.
A butterfly's gossamer wing.
Things I hold in my heart
when life looks bleak.

Make me pause each day to
remember these bountiful blessings.
Soften my heart when
small slights distract me.

Make me worthy of Your grace
as I live every day.

- Ruth Williams

Recognition of Beauty

I won't spend one more day in fear.
Today I will not be limited by
negative thoughts that gobble up the day
and don't allow me
to recognize the beauty around me.

Today I will be freed of unrealistic expectations
that lead to disappointment and self-pity.

I am committed to being in the moment
where I am safe, provided for and loved.

- Robyn Cruze

Galpals

They're the ones
that I can count on,
sure as the beads on an abacus.
It is miraculous to me
how You fit them into my life:
the childhood friend,
the college roommate,
the confidante,
the sisters by birth
and by marriage.
Treasures, all…
a profusion much greater
than one woman deserves.
Thank You for the bonds
forged by women's hearts,
for tangible evidence
of Your enduring love.
Knowing You could not
be present in flesh,
You sent me those
who can and are.

- Lori Strawn

Coming to You in Prayer

Help me lift my mind
and heart to You.
Let me come in reverence,
for You are greater
than anything else can be.
Let me raise my voice in thanks,
for You have given me so much.
Let me hold up my brothers and sisters,
fellow humans,
in need of Your love,
Your strength
and Your mercy.
And last of all,
let me share with You
my own concerns
for You are the One
who listens when I pray
and holds my cares close
day and night.

- Sue Bradford Edwards

Walk Away Gently

I cannot love him.
Not the way he is asking me to.

When I look at him,
I see what a masterpiece
You have made —
an admirable mind,
a kind spirit,
a man deserving of genuine,
unrestrained love.

You have given me enough
understanding to see
that it is time to walk away.
Now I ask for the wisdom
to help him understand,
to speak tenderly,
without condescending,
to speak honestly,
without hurting him needlessly,
and to walk away with the peace of knowing
that I gave another human being
the best I was able to give —
even if it was less than he asked for.

When it is over,
stay with us both.
Bring us comfort and peace,
that we may find in You the completion
we could not find in one another.

- Abigail Wurdeman

Inside / Outside

Did you ever feel the need to flee?
To leave, give into
An overwhelming flight response,
Not knowing where you might go?

Do we think that just by altering
The direction we are headed
That somehow we will change
The outcome that we fear?

Divine intervention will always
Supersede any plan
That we might have.
Like your shadow, it is yours forever.

What if we stayed, feet planted firm
In deep resolve and let You stay our course?
Would the end result be the same?
I have learned through many lessons, yes.

Let me know Your will,
Your heart's desire, my own now.
Train me; prune me, in the faith life
That I may bear fruit pleasing to You.

Inside, show me how to love unconditionally,
Free to express Your words
Of comfort and tolerance;
Let compassion fill my soul, overflowing.

Outside, let my touch be Yours,
Healing those who hunger for it.
Make my arms instruments of Your
Grace as I comfort in Your name.

Inside, outside let me be,
Until You lay me down to rest,
An expression of Your boundless love…

- Heidi Haller

Self-Acceptance

I achieved Rubenesque status
by eating reubens,
living life fully, indulging to the hilt.
Fondly, I remember fondue.
The bakery, sacred to me.
I approach pie with what one
can only regard as piety.

Thank You for this ample frame,
which allowed me to
nurse a child, embrace a lover,
envelop friends with warmth,
carry the weight of the world on my shoulders.

Thank You for this, shall we say, "Largess,"
which makes even a wooden chair comfortable,
since I carry my own cushion on my person.
Thank You for the tincture of time and the wisdom of years,
which makes me appreciate my fullness — fully.
Now, pass the pasta.

- Ruth Williams

Humility

Humble me.
Make me small enough to fit
on the head of a pin,
lest I believe
that Your deeds are mine.
All the good I accomplish
pours forth from You;
I am merely a vessel.
And when I know this fully,
there will be no diminishment,
only awe.

- Lori Strawn

Trust the Connections

When and where
I will connect with You
isn't something I can predict;
yet I judge when and where
others will make these connections.

Only with You
can I lead without pushing,
wait without impatience and
give others the space
to find You wherever
You are in their day and
in the world.

In me, You see possibility.
Please help me see others
through Your eyes,
to love others
through Your heart,
to not place my own limitations
on their possibilities.

- Sue Bradford Edwards

Work It Out

Everything is already worked out.
Every sorrow, every heartache,
every problem, every unpaid bill.
I won't try to figure it out.

Nothing is left undone.
All is for my good.
I thank You for wiping my tears,
reminding me I am not alone.
Prosperity is mine.

- Brenda Scott

Bless This Mess

If cleanliness is next to godliness,
this house is in another zip code.
Divine presence, please bless our dirty home,
for it has been lived in and loved in.
Thank you for every messy inch of it.

For the dust lining the shelves,
crowded with books I have read and loved.
For dishes in the sink that yielded up something yummy.
For the scattering of shoes that prove
my house is full of people I love.
And yes, even for whatever it is the cat hacked up on the sofa.

Thank You for giving us a home to wreck.
And thank You —
oh so fervently —
for making it Your home, too.

- Lori Strawn

Scared

I look to You when I am scared.
I am scared now.
I ask for Your peace to cradle my soul,
to enfold me within Your warmth,
understanding and grace.

I ask for Your strength to filter
within me and to help me spread courage
among those who are also frightened.

Answer me and provide me with
Your loving and safe embrace.

- Karen Laven

Through Your Eyes

Today, tomorrow and always,
may I be allowed to see everyone
I come in contact with
through Your eyes.

When they speak out in anger,
let me see the hurt
that consumes them,
the anguish that shields their tears.

Let me be the reassuring voice
that heals, giving me Your words.
Let me see that a human touch
can save another human being.

Let me see the stranger
who You created out of love,
replacing their needs
over my own.

Let me see how the world
was meant to be,
through Your eyes, now and forever.

- Heidi Haller

Your Presence Requested

I know You're there, but where?
Worries are poking at me, sharp-clawed:
my job, my family, my life.
I can't feel You today, and I am afraid.
Where are You?
Please make Yourself present —
clear and tangible —
let me feel You near me
in the common moments of my life,
in my breathing and being,
in my most terrifying and trying times.
Take my fears away.
Help me go past them, to peace.

- Lori Strawn

Transparency

I am not perfect.
I want to be able to discover
the needs and wants of others.
I should not have felt
those things in my heart
or said the wrong thing.
I have demonstrated
that I am not transparent
and I don't listen.
I am not perfect.

You created me to have
a personal relationship with You.
I hear You whisper:
Feel generously
Speak kindly
Live openly.
Intimacy means being close to You,
by listening to You.

- Brenda Scott

Seventh Day

Sometimes the answer
is in the waiting…
sometimes the answer is, be still.
Pause. Breathe.
For Whoever crafted nature,
tiny toddler toes,
and worlds without end
is surely able.

And if the seventh day
was the day of rest,
Then no matter
how much world-shifting,
life-changing drama may be
in the offing,
there's always
the seventh day.

Please remind me of this,
as I run in place,
and shake my fist at the sky.
Respite, relief, and rest will come.
Be present for me even
when I am not myself,
and help me to calm my mind.

- Ruth Williams

You Know

Only You can say what I need.
I think I know: this job, that house,
this person that I say I love.
But only You can say what I need.

I do know what I want:
to trust more in You,
in the gentle and hopeful
unveiling of Your promise.

- Miranda Claudius

Understanding 101

Lost amongst my acres of knowledge
and mounds of books,
I'm a mere academic,
trying to make sense of life and love.

I own a mellifluous mountain
of meandering meaningless words,
and I mouth them
when the moment arises.

I cannot tell the difference between
patois, idiolect, jargon, dialect,
idiom, argot, slang, and gobbledygook,
or colloquialism, waffle, claptrap.

I care not for ephemeral sounds;
"I'm sorry; I don't speak your vernacular."
I pray for someone to understand me.

- Tanja Cilia

Finding Time

It's everywhere.
Sitting on the bus
or driving in the car.
Waiting at the deli counter,
number 56 in hand.
Who knew 3 pounds
of lean corned beef
could get me closer
to the promised land?

Trapped inside the dentist's chair,
my eyes glued shut,
I give my heartfelt thanks,
and it doesn't hurt as much.

Finding time to pray
is not as hard as I thought.
Whether I'm kneeling in front of my bed,
or elbow-deep in soapsuds
at the kitchen sink,
You hear me, always.

- Karen Laven

The Hike

The world seems endless.
The hills rolling on below and around me,
the trees tall and unbending
from here to the horizon and beyond.

I see You.
I see the work of Your hands,
I hear the sound of Your voice,
I feel Your breath
soft and cool on my skin.

With You here at my side,
my strained muscles relax,
my hurried breath slows,
my racing heart calms.

And I rest,
in harmony with Your world,
alive in Your Presence.

- Abigail Wurdeman

Change is Coming

I feel like I have fallen
and I can't get up.
Source of my strength, lift me.
Change is coming.

My dreams and visions are shattered.
Source of my strength,
put it all back together.
Change is coming.

Everything I think is right,
is turned upside down.
Source of my strength,
fix the wrongs.
Change is coming.

Source of my strength,
I need You now.
Change is coming.

- Brenda Scott

Urban Dweller

Among skyscrapers and city streets,
You are here.
I sense You in sun-hot pavement,
glinting glass and rumbling buses.
When I take the train,
I see You in the faces of Your children —
young and old, men and women, from all lands.

You are here.

- Sue Bradford Edwards

Providence

Call it kismet or divine intervention —
I am where I need to be.
Let me never forget
that I did not wander here
unplanned by chance.
You led me to this place.
I am on stage awaiting my cue.
What can I do for You here?
With whom can I connect?
Let me do Your work and will,
and we shall move together
to the next destination.
Only You know my destiny,
though I know this:
In providence, I am never lost.

- Lori Strawn

This Garment

The one I love is on my mind.
I carry him with me every day,
like a shawl that covers me,
or a stone in my pocket
that I constantly reach for
to make sure it's still there.

But I worry so much about our future.
It's unknown, like everyone's.
It's riddled with questions.
I know pockets can rip,
stones can fall through,
and uncertainty wear us down
leaving only a frayed cloth after time.

Help me to listen to You and to him.
Help me to trust in Your steady hand,
in that patient sewing of our lives.

- Miranda Claudius

Paso Doble

Each day is a blessing
of epic proportions.
I give thanks for
what might seem meager comforts:
real cream in my coffee,
a day without a bill in the mail,
Paso Doble, the Spanish two-step.
Sometimes life is a dance
a woman has to do backwards
pushing against the wind
and obstacles in the way.
Thank You for being the partner
who always leads.

- Ruth Williams

After the Dark

At the end of the day
my eyes are tired.
My sadness is heavy.
The nights tightening quiet
gives me much time to worry.

But following that silence
You bring gifts of noise:
morning rain, coffee percolators,
school buses stopping on the corner.

And these life-giving sounds
appear to remind me:
You are the one
to bring this new day.
You give these moments
that fill me with hope.

- Miranda Claudius

Au Fait

You know every sole
that has ever left a footprint in the sand.
You know every child
who has ever flown home from college
to spend a holiday with their family.
You know every Scout leader
that has hiked a forest trail.

You know them all, and You hear them all,
even as You know me, and hear me,
and hold me in the palm of Your hand.
Even when I think I am alone, You are there.
You know us all.

- Sue Bradford Edwards

Divine Moments

I feel You within me like never before.
My trust in You has paid off.
This is contentment.

Splendid, astounding,
worth every prayer,
every heartache, sublime serenity.
A solid finite companion, not by my side,
but inside my being, a part of my soul.

Ahhhh, I savor You,
I savor this blessed moment of bliss.

- Karen Laven

Stepping Back

Please help me to step back
from the rush and clamor
of day-to-day life.
Help me to disconnect
if only for a few moments
so that I may sit quietly
and do nothing but breathe.
In this way, may I find the space
and the time to feel Your presence.
To connect with the well-spring of peace
that comes only through
that which is greater than myself.

- Sue Bradford Edwards

Appoggiatura

In Italian there is a
lingering note that precedes
the fugue of living.
Appoggiatura — a sustained tone
that cuts into the time
of the next chord.
Sometimes it's called a grace note,
alternately, a time-stealer.

There's a whole constellation
of distractions in my repertoire.
Things I tell myself
I must accomplish before
I let joy settle:
That last ten pounds
That college degree
That nest egg.

Please help me take
Your words to heart —
that grace is a gift,
and life is to be lived.
Right now.

- Ruth Williams

Gifted

Others praise You
with voices raised in song.
Still others paint awe-inspiring
canvases or raise buildings into the sky.
Let me praise You with the talents
You have given me.

I can reach out a hand
to steady my elderly neighbor,
or raise my heart in prayer
for a sorrowing friend.

I can stir a pot bubbling on the stove
as I wait for my hungry spouse.
I can speak comfort to a discouraged teen or
smile at the mother of an energetic child.

In all these ways,
I praise You,
who made me as I am.

- Sue Bradford Edwards

Friendly Aging

Walk with me,
even when my back aches.
Remind me of the gift
of my good health.
Allow me to return the favor,
by sharing my time
with those in need.
It's a blessing to begin
my golden years and know
I'm never really alone.
Thank You for letting me
age with my friends,
so none of us notices we're getting older.

- Ruth Williams

Rock Me Slowly

Today, he closed the door behind him,
all he wanted, in his suitcase.
Upstairs, an empty bed once shared.
A table holds the gifts I gave him;
more closet space, I cannot fill.

Still holding up, and holding on.
I turned to see — he left our photos.
The dam burst, tears flooding,
inconsolable, I cry out,
"This will be my undoing!"

You, my Creator, sustain me
in my darkest hour.
Lift me up and rock me slowly.

You, who know my path ahead,
tell me, tomorrow I will push past.

Help me heal, reliving only memories
that offer up a smile.
I commit to You and I trust in You.
Someday, I will feel whole again.

- Heidi Haller

Standing Tall

The moment is still.
The news is frightful.
I watch her rise
and exit the room.
Behind her a prediction
of failure, of sickness,
a future far from easy.
I want to glance away
and forget her face.

But no — steel my stare.
Help me look even closer
and remember only this:

A woman's spirit
is not measured
by the rooms of doubt
she may walk through,
but by how she enters
the rest of her world.

- Miranda Claudius

Words Do Hurt

If only I could take them back!
But the words flew
out of my thoughtless mouth
like a bullet out of a gun.
I watched it pierce,
the pain welling up in my friend's eyes.
I felt it ricochet through me, too,
gutting me to the heart.
There seems no end to the ways
that words can harm.
I, alone, cannot fix this.

Dear friend, the only friend
my cruelty can never alienate:
I ask You for forgiveness.
I ask You to give me the right words,
words to mend fences,
words to patch wounds,
words to repair what has been broken.
Open my friend's heart
that she might receive my apology.
And slow my tongue in future,
that I might never wound again.

- Lori Strawn

Let It Ring

I woke this morning in America,
and I know what freedom is.

Where there is injustice,
I am free to fight.
Where there is silence,
I am free to speak,
Where there is hate,
I am free to love.

And when I grope in the darkness for understanding,
I am free to seek the light —
I am free to find You.

Thank You for this bold and open-hearted nation,
and for the bold and open-hearted leaders who protect
my life of precious liberty.
Tonight, my soul explodes with praise,
my joy bursting its colors against the night sky.

- Abigail Wurdeman

The Gift

Let me give not only of my resources,
but also of my spirit.
May the kernel light of goodwill within me
be made greater with the giving,
radiating outward,
passing from fingertip to fingertip,
each kindness kindling another.
May every hand learn the warmth of fellowship
to receive in need and to give in prosperity —
passing the flame ever forward,
until all the world is awash in the brilliant light of giving.

- Abigail Wurdeman

Women of All Faiths

We gather together,
women of all faiths.
We bring to you
our thanks and our worries,
our joy and our heartbreak.
You are much greater
than we can ever be.
Please share with us
the peace and wisdom
You give to all who ask.
Give us hope and joy
as we gather together
today and tomorrow.

- Sue Bradford Edwards

Immeasurable Grace

Stopped at a corner in my car
saw a man holding a sign.
It read, I'm hungry.
You say, "Feed him."

Walked by a woman
sleeping on a cardboard box.
She needed warmth.
You say, "Cover her."

Crossed through a parking lot;
there was an elderly lady
carrying heavy bags.
You say, "Ease her burden."

I long to grow closer to You
for your ways to be my ways.
You who feed,
provide comfort,
carry burdens.
Let me be a reflection of
Your immeasurable grace.

- Heidi Haller

Peace Plea

Please, protect my child.
Please, protect other mothers' children.
Please, give me peace.
Please, give other mothers peace.
Please, give the world peace.
This is the peace only You can give.

- Karen Laven

Three-Legged Stool

I feel You when
people do good deeds for the needy.
I see You when
society opens a checkbook to serve others.
I hear You when
citizens speak out for justice.

May Your spirit settle upon the many
who look to make this world a better place.

- Rachel Lee

Broadcast

Help me silence the relentless roar
of newscasters and fanatics.
So much of what we hear each day
seeks to separate us from one another.
I watch the news because I want to know
what is going on in the world.
What I see and hear is hate.

Help me look into the faces around me
and see the divine spark You have given
each and every one of us.
Help me, and women like me,
who come to You seeking comfort,
singing praise, bring
Your peace and love into the world.

- Sue Bradford Edwards

Touchstone

Please remind me that my heart
has only four chambers.
Scant room for such squatters
as grudges, slights, pettiness.
If I carry around baggage from the past,
there isn't room for blessings unbounded.

Help me to disarm unilaterally,
so it isn't possible to engage
in anything but joy.
So I turn over my weapons to You.
Help me be serene in a world with
such oxymorons as peace-keeping missiles.
Help me release my faith: World peace is possible.
My peace is here.

- Ruth Williams

Job Over

We never saw it coming.
He opened up his paycheck.
Pink slip.
Laid off.
Shocked, we held each other.

Nine months later, savings gone.
A house we love,
we must leave.
Stack of bills
we can't pay.
I tell myself I can't do this.
Falling to my knees, I sob.

I need You more than ever;
with You, I can face this.
Please, help me up.

You, who supplies the courage,
tenacity, and promise,
help me gather up my faith
and follow You.
My rock,
My hope.

- Heidi Haller

Entrepreneur

I am waiting and waiting.
I am always getting ready.
Standing in this unemployment line,
I know I must renew my strength.
I have to go out and get what I want.
I have to make opportunities for myself.
You gave me a vision for a new business —
show me how to create it.
I will never receive all that You have for me
if I keep waiting and getting ready.
I praise You while I move forward
toward the unique purpose
You have created for me.

- Brenda Scott

Wisdom of Our Elders

Bless the Nanas of the world,
the Pop-Pops, the Gramps,
who show us how to knit, how to fish,
how to find a good mood
even when their sciatica kicks in.

Secretly holding the world together,
they don't compete
with whoever the Joneses might be,
and teach that kindness
is love on a slow drip.

Release that spirit in me today.

Help me to emulate them:
Slow boiling point,
story at the ready,
candy and kind word in pocket.

Very few things in life are so aptly named.
There's a reason we call them "grand."

- Ruth Williams

This Amazing Soul

Today, I look upon
our newborn child;
I stare with complete joy
and utter fear.
Joy, because this amazing soul
leaves me breathless with wonder.
Perfect in ways
I never dreamed possible.
But I also feel intense fear.
The responsibility of instilling
tolerance, patience, love and faith
in a world that is starving
for all these virtues.

I feel inadequate.
Can I measure up to what is required of me?
Yes, I feel your presence —
immense calmness.
Knowing You reside inside of me.
You have allowed me to glimpse
at what You must have felt,
during the creation of our universe.

- Heidi Haller

You, Everywhere

Who knew You could be present
in the mopping of a floor?
But there You are.
I find You, too,
next to the bread
as I fix his brown bag sandwich.
And there You are,
riding shotgun, as I rush to the store
to pick up that prescription.

You are always there,
just to one side of my busy day,
like divine peripheral vision.
What can I give You in return?
I have only me,
and it seems a poor gift.
But here it is, gladly given.
I love You.

- Lori Strawn

Apology

When night stretches endless,
I call out for You.
When day turns gray and lonely
I long for You.
When I am sick,
my breath growing ragged and painful,
I cling to You.
But when I am immersed in joy,
I forget You.
I am sorry.

- Lori Strawn

Knowing I am Home

This place is not quite home,
but soon enough it will be.
And it all begins with You.

Come inside.
Live with me here.
Surround me in these walls.
Guard me with this roof.
Support me with these floorboards.
Be in the food that I eat.
Sit among the guests I entertain.
Let me lie down beside You
at the end of each day and
wake to your perfect light each morning.

Be part of every board and rafter,
every knob and faucet.
Knowing You are here means knowing I am home.

- Abigail Wurdeman

Daughter of the Woods

I go to the woods, for You are there.
You, fully in attendance
in every leaf and bough,
replenish my soul
with the sigh of the wind.

I come here to be with You,
where You dwell most presently,
to spin out the contents of my heart,
and be regaled
with green-black silences
and the living canopy
of nature's cathedral.

I go to the woods to recharge,
to drink my fill of You.
Please —
grow a forest in my heart
that I might carry You everywhere.

- Lori Strawn

What Love Says

Love says:
You are the one who believes
that I will never find you.
But I am searching, searching only for you.
If only you'd realize that I reside in that place
where you never seem to look.

Love says:
Listen, go inside yourself.
Search yourself,
like you're looking for a secret,
or the answer to your life.
Fall deep inside.
Find me there.
I will hold your ankles,
make sure you get back out.

- Miranda Claudius

Making Way for Clarity

Thank You for clearing:
my mind,
my vision,
my arteries,
my conscience,
the road ahead of me.
Thank You for
the clarity that
I have but to ask for.

- Ruth Williams

For All the Single Ladies

I grew up believing that
every princess finds her prince.
It's inevitable.

My kingdom, on the other hand,
is full of frogs.
No matter how often I kiss them,
they remain stubbornly amphibious.

Where is the prince You made for me?
Help me find him.
Fish him out of this sea of possibilities.
My life remains Your tale to tell.

I remain ever-hopeful,
ever-trusting in Your narration.
Please grant me my happily ever after,
after all.

- Lori Strawn

Priorities

I can do it all
(I've told myself);
I've got lists.
Yet, why do I sometimes forget to talk to You?
Were You not on my list?

Help me to keep You at the top of my list,
to keep my priorities in line:
You,
family,
friends,
community,
career.

Help me remember, I cannot always do it all;
only You can.
Help me to do whatever I do
with You ever-most in my mind.

- Karen Laven

You Are All

From the vastness of the universe
full of darkness,
stars and infinite space,
to the tiny wonder of one small seed
cradled in dark soil,
bathed in spring rain,
waiting to grow.
You are in it all.
It is all in You.

From the ice of winter,
sparkling, waiting, quiet.
To the green of summer,
insects thrumming,
scent pulsing from the fields.
You are in it all.
It is all in You.

From the smiling wonder
of a baby reaching out
with a plump hand,
eager to explore,
to the smiling wonder
of an elder enjoying a sunny day,
remembering similar days.
You are in it all.
It is all in You.

- Sue Bradford Edwards

Muses

As I sit musing, I wonder,
where does inspiration come from?
Everything distracts me
as I work at my desk:
the indigo flame of sunset
out my window,
a sweet fur ball of a dog with the bark
of Darth Vader asking for a belly rub,
the joyboy padding down the hall,
sleep in his starsize eyes,
Bach's Air on G,
wafting through my home.

My mind wanders to the fresh crusty bread
waiting in the kitchen.
The crock-pot filled with noodles, chicken, carrots.
Nothing to inspire me on the page today!
Too much good to wade through in my life.
Glory be.

Thank You for my muses and the music of my life.
Please continue to rain blessings
on me and all who enter my home.

- Ruth Williams

Child Inside Me

I don't wanna.
I don't wanna get out of bed,
take a shower,
make breakfast.
I don't wanna iron my shirt,
drive to work,
sit in that blasted cubby all day.

You understand,
I do wish I'd wanna.
With Your help, I will
make the most of my day.
I won't disappoint me,
my children,
my boss,
or more importantly,
You.

- Karen Laven

Danse Macabre

It gets better.
Stay in between my synapses
tap it out in Morse code
if need be.

It gets better.
Take me outside to look
at the birds flying in unison
taste the salty air
by the boundless ocean
feel the sand between clenched toes.

It gets better.
Take my mind off what I know
is too big for me
this thing I always dance around
and never mention.

That's why there is faith.
It's the bridge between
the impossible and the infinite.
Please get me and mine safely across.

- Ruth Williams

Listening

Your voice is like the rain
that gently hits the roof of my car.
It's a song asking me
to open a door
and exit. Get up. Move on.
Rise from there and laugh again.

But all I want to do,
for just now,
is sit inside and listen.

You make everything new again.

- Miranda Claudius

Rubber Meets Road

Every day without fail,
I tell my son: Always do the right thing.
If you give your word, keep it.

Sometimes he rolls his eyes,
but I know it sinks in eventually.

I look back at the fading
forensics of those times
You tried to reach me too.
Rolling my eyes toward the heavens, I tuned You out.

Look at the whole of nature and the arc of life and it's clear:
I gave you my word, and I'll keep it.

Please make me mindful of the fact
That the things that really matter find their way back in time.

- Ruth Williams

Thanks to You

I give You thanks for carrying me through
the muckiest patches of life.
Emerging with scratches, yes;
but they pale compared to the
faith-filled ferocity of my inner power.

I give You thanks for bestowing within me
the determination to stand tall, not back away
and run from overbearing pain and fear.
(I wanted to flee, at first.
I thank You for not letting me.)

I give You thanks for giving me perspective
to grasp what is most important in this realm
and to let flutter away the inconsequential.
I give You thanks for still being here to give You thanks.

- Karen Laven

The Reason

Prayer is a gift I give myself.
I turn to You,
because then I am not alone.
I give You my troubles:
You can bear them.
I give You my thanks:
You grant me all my needs.
I give You my praise:
You give me more to admire.
I get more than I can ever give.
And that is why I pray.

- Lori Strawn

You, Me, and the Lamp Post

Just between us —
I've done things I wouldn't want
to see in the headlines,
so I won't be throwing
a stone in your direction.
Every dark alley,
each "partner in crime,"
all of it weighs on my soul.
Checkered past? Try paisley.
Thank You for the mornings after
and the sinking feelings.

Please remind me
that even though all of that is behind me,
I must never forget
that my house is made of glass.
A full wall of windows:
Looking in, you can see my past
and permanent record.
Looking out, there's only the clearest day
and glistening grace.

- Ruth Williams

Sensing Grace

I finally sense the grace
that is at my grasp every day.
It is here.

When it's frigid,
when it's bleak,
when I'm joyous.
It is here.

When health suffers,
when loved ones pass,
when I'm grateful.
It is here.
When hearts ache,
when fear festers,
when I'm content.
It is here.

It is here, because
You are here.

- Karen Laven

Office of Empathy

Years ago, I would never have felt this way.
Thank You for the darkest days.
It infused me with an understanding
I wouldn't otherwise have.

Life is something I must learn on the job;
empathy is earned.
I can tell someone, "I know how you feel,"
or I can actually live through it
and graduate to authenticity.

It's the scars and the stumbles that make it real
as I reach out to someone else.
Thanks to the depression, the divorce, the dangers,
I'm uniquely equipped for the Office of Empathy.

- Ruth Williams

Just Desserts

I knew I shouldn't…
even before I ate it.
But it was so tempting,
so delicious, so mine.
I say I want to lose weight;
I know what it takes — really.
I do know, but somehow
I can't bring myself to try.

Help me understand why I am
hiding behind these extra pounds.
Help me love myself
as You love me.
Help me see myself worth
the effort it will take.

Let me remember
that I am worthy
and loved by You.

- Sue Bradford Edwards

Seek and You Will Find

There's a lesson in here somewhere.
It's in everything I do,
but camouflaged as it must be.
I hunt for Your clues along the way.

Through waiting, I learn patience
and the meaning of Your timing.
Through loss, I find everything
that's more important then I thought.

Disappointment teaches me
that what is lost
must hold Your values —
not of this world, but the next.

In happiness, I now can see
life's smallest pleasures
as sweets to share with others
so they may feed their souls.

Please continue to open my eyes
to look earnestly for Your meanings.
Make me be Your student,
unrelenting, in my quest for truths.

For only then can Your answers
be revealed to me.
I seek You with all my heart.
You do not hide, but point the way.

- Heidi Haller

Small Wonders

I praise You for the tiny glories
I am often too busy to see:
the irregular scallop of a maple leaf,
the impossible yellow of a dandelion,
the perfection of untrammeled snow.

For the scrap of sunlight the cat finds
in the darkened hallway,
I thank You.

For each sudden splendor:
the tickle of grass,
the dizzying dome of sky after rain,
the cozy smell of someone I love,
I exalt You.
Your beauty bursts my heart.

- Lori Strawn

Acknowledgements

The editor would like to acknowledge everyone who made this book possible: Susan Diamond, whose big idea brought Prayables to life; her indispensable right hand gal, Amanda Rinker; technological genius Ed Eusebio who developed and manages our website; my gifted fellow writers on the Pray Makers Council, Ruth Williams, Heidi Haller, Sue Bradford Edwards, Karen Laven and Brenda Scott; and all of the talented women who contributed their prayers to Prayables.com. For believing in a world where women of all faiths can come together in prayer, I thank you.

Personal Prayer Pages